Asymmetrical Resistance Manual

Extraordinary Difficulties Demand Extraordinary Action

Distribute this manual freely by whatever means possible. We can't let the sociopaths continue to make life miserable for the rest of us.

Do the most good, for the most people, most often.

ISBN-13: 978-1983757655

ISBN-10: 1983757659

Table of Contents

Asymmetrical Resistance Manual [ARM]

Every discussion begins with an agreement of terms. Here are a few of the terms and what they mean in this document.

Asymmetrical = having parts that fail to correspond to one another in shape, size, or arrangement; lacking symmetry.

Resistance = a secret organization resisting authority, the refusal to accept or comply with something.

Random Act of Kindness = A surprise act of kindness that the recipient has little or no chance of returning.

Manual = a book of instructions.

Method = orderliness of thought or behavior; systematic planning or action.

Member = an individual belonging to a group such as a society or team.

Tripod = Basic operational unit of the Asymmetrical Resistance Method. Tripods are more thoroughly discussed under the section called "Tripods" later in this document. You will see this term referenced a few times before getting to that section. If you find it difficult to understand what is being discussed, it might be helpful to skip ahead to that section and return after reading it.

"The Machine" = regimes, usually controlled by mentally ill sociopaths, that operate for the shortsighted benefit of a few to the detriment of everyone else. It is any organization, private or public, that acts against the interest of humanity.

Artifact = Something, usually small enough to be unseen, dismissed or ignored, that is not naturally present but that is artificially introduced to cause the Machine to malfunction or operate differently than intended.

The 3Ms = Do the most good, for the most people, most often.

The Concept

"The Machine" feeds on the blood of the people. Being sociopathic at its core, it thrives on fear and hate. The Machine injects fear into people at every opportunity. Fear inspires hate. It thrives on people fearing and hating one another. "The Machine's" dessert is people fearing it.

Ironically when people hold large demonstrations as a show of hatred for "Machines", it's a feast or carnival for these "Machines". They have a bounty of heads to bash. They can indiscriminately cause mayhem to many people while watching people get killed or injured, burning down their own neighborhoods and looting the few businesses that service their communities. These sociopaths will be vicariously licking the blood from their mouths.

The asymmetrical resistance strategy is aimed at minimizing damage to people and property. It is aimed at asymmetrically neutralizing and repurposing these machines.

Because The Machine has many weak points, there are many ways to attack those weak points. The more you research and understand how the machine works, how it gets its power and where its vulnerabilities are, the more opportunities you will have to attack those vulnerable points at the least cost of blood and suffering to the people you are trying to help.

Listing all or even most of the ways it can be done would be counterproductive since we must assume that The Machine has a copy of this document and/or dossiers on most, if not all, of the people using it.

Machines have a difficult time with asymmetry. They need to find a pattern in order to operate. The power of asymmetry is that it complicates the process of finding that pattern. Instead of hiding a needle in a haystack, asymmetric resistance hides the needle in a stack of other needles.

If you hide a needle in a haystack, the needle is different enough in properties from hay that it can rather easily be extracted, with a magnet for example. However, in a pile of other needles, the task becomes much more difficult. This is hiding in plain view. Hiding in plain view is almost invisible.

This is to say that there are few advantages in labeling your activities as an Asymmetrical Resistance Method or mentioning you have a Tripod. Those who belong to your pod will know you. Even others who are following the

Asymmetrical Resistance Method can cooperate with you fully without advertising that they are part of a Tripod. It is not about "identity" or ego, it is about getting results.

Asymmetric resistance finds its strength in subtlety and anonymity. Its power comes from doing things that we all do or should do all of the time with slight twists.

That said, a template with some useful examples of asymmetric resistance might be useful. These are offered as starting points. It is expected that you will be perpetually creative once you understand the basic concept. This method of resistance relies on the creativity of its users.

The purpose of this manual is to offer actions that individuals and small groups can take to thwart oppressive organizations that sometimes pose as governments. It is the belief of the author that all actions by all people should be based on the 3Ms. The 3Ms represent the gold standard of whether something is worthy of support by humans. It measures attitudes and actions of the degree to which a person, politician, policy, law, act, or product does the MOST good, for the MOST people, MOST often.

The Asymmetrical Resistance Method [ARM] is designed to help the most people, take the most effective action, most often with the least amount of exposure to blow back by oppressive regimes. It is not thought of as fool-proof. It is not designed to get quick action. It is designed to cut like water through a canyon. It is designed to morph into the environment in such a way as to be barely perceptible while disrupting, disabling and repurposing organizations that do not serve the principles of the 3Ms: doing the most good, for the most people, most of the time.

Doing the most good for the most people most of the time is a theme that is at the basis of both the goals and tactics of this effort. The people who use this approach to social change are called on to keep this idea at the top of their thoughts and actions at all times. It should be their mantra. It should become a lifestyle. It should in time become effortless and just a part of what one does and who one is. Doing the most good for the most people most of the time will empower them and their actions.

It should become a part of one's life so that others experience it as who the person is. This approach to creating positive social and political change seeks to make actual change at the personal and grass roots levels that will neutralize the power of oppressive regimes operated by sociopaths, i.e. "The Machine", to make life miserable for most people most of the time.

This approach recognizes that, while mass demonstrations certainly have an important place in the fight for social and political change arena, The Machine knows that people are hurt by its actions but does not care. Demonstrations do not bring new information to The Machine. Mass demonstrations often have the down side of placing the people who oppose The Machine, in a vulnerable position, making it easy for The Machine to punish them together for their opposition.

This approach offers an alternative method of resistance intended as a critical addition or alternative to demonstrations. It is not a matter of either/or but both/and. Do whatever you can that you feel will do the most good for the most people most of the time.

This approach seeks to create change at such a fundamental, personal and community level that The Machine even participates in its own change. This approach seeks to starve The Machine of its primary fuels: fear, mistrust, hatred. This approach seeks to repurpose the material resources of The Machine to serve the needs of the many.

Because this approach operates "invisibly in plain view" it has no heroes. It draws power from anonymity. It largely operates within what looks to be the scope of "normal" human activities. While making small changes that nudge human activities in directions that make it difficult to impossible for The Machine to operate, it seeks to neutralize sociopathy at the personal and systemic levels. It blunts and weakens the The Machine's weapons of violence and deprivation.

While this can feel a bit cloak and dagger, the concept is to be invisible in plain view. Much of the most important work involves taking barely perceptible but effective action. For example, one can smile or commit a random act of kindness hundreds of times a day. These acts can be imperceptible in the grand scheme of things, but they grind away at the bitterness and loneliness that fuel The Machine. These smiles are the waves that wash away the sand castles of sociopaths.

About 4% of the human population can be clinically diagnosed as sociopathic. These mentally and emotionally disturbed people simply lack the ability to feel empathy for others. To better understand this please read, "The Sociopath Next Door" by Martha Stout.

This small minority of people has imposed the effects of their mental illness on the rest of us. They are likely to be the cause of most of the self-inflicted human suffering throughout history.

It is largely these mentally ill people who hurt people. Hurt people, hurt people. They are the ones who promote the idea that it is "natural" to harm or kill others in order to survive or "make progress". These sociopaths create fake lines between people based on religion, "race", ethnicity or other "identities". While we search for a cure for this mental illness, we must neutralize their ability to manipulate the rest of us into making ourselves miserable for their entertainment. This approach is about limiting or eliminating the power of the 4% to harm to the rest of us.

The Asymmetrical Resistance Method is intended to operate locally, but have global impact. Much of the strategy is organized around "tripods". The tripod is the basic operational unit of this approach. It will be discussed in more detail a little later.

However, the Asymmetrical Resistance Method can also be implemented by a "lone operator". That is to say, as many of the tactics become a lifestyle, they can and should be carried out in random, asymmetrical patterns. And since the practitioners do not stand out, they should be able to operate in plain view, even while appearing to want to cooperate with The Machine.

Some microorganisms use this strategy of defense. They make their DNA appear to the host to be the host's DNA. The host is then unable to attack the organism because it cannot distinguish the organism from itself.

Sociopaths use this strategy on the rest of us. They make us think that their interests are our interests. They divide us by making us think we must "defend our 'race,'" when we are really only defending their narrow personal interest. They make us think we must defend "our god and religion" while they set themselves up as God's exclusive mouth piece and act like they are on a first name basis with God or even Gods themselves. They make us think we must invade the homelands of others and/or support economic systems that exploit and deprive most of us while they are really the only ones who benefit. Knowing how they operate creates an opportunity to neutralize their power to make people miserable.

The Asymmetrical Resistance Method can be low tech or high tech. It can utilize massive resources, but is only dependent on the human resources of will power and a desire to create one human family free of control of sociopaths, aka the 4% or "The Machine".

Much of the power of the Asymmetrical Resistance Method comes from crowd sourcing. While it is based on small units of "tripods", its power comes from crowd sourcing. By interacting with "the crowd" in small groups, change can be made on the "cellular level" of the "organism". What people experience on a daily basis will affect how they consume information and directives from alien sources like mass media.

Machines depend on a stable environment. They need a high degree of predictability. They have difficulty adjusting to change. Machines try to force us into predictable patterns because they need us to be predictable to control us. Being unpredictable, random, and asymmetrical is key to the success of the Asymmetrical Resistance Method. This manual is aimed at providing the structure that will allow readers to create their own tactics. It is a starting point. It should be embellished, keeping with the core objective of doing the most good, for the most people, most often.

Small focused changes plus time can immobilize machines. Small focused asymmetrical changes to the machine and/or its environment can cause the machine to self-destruct.

The goal of the asymmetrical resistance movement is to empower people to defend themselves against The Machine and neutralize or eliminate power used against people, in a way that minimizes harm to people or destruction of property. Since it is quite effective it must be used with great discretion. Misused, it could harm the very people it is meant to help. Used indiscriminately, it could potentially make civilization an historic relic.

That said, it is time to end the misery caused by sociopaths that causes the rest of humanity to suffer. We need to quarantine these mentally ill people from any sources of power until we can find a cure for their mental illness. We must take control of our lives from those who sow fear, hatred and division. We cannot let the 4% continue to cause the rest of us to suffer.

Make no mistake. This method is not easy. It is not quick. But it can be fun. It should be fun. It will be effective.

Tripods

Tripods are the basic operational units of the Asymmetrical Resistance Method (ARM). It is composed of three "legs", each of which is composed of three people, plus one "head" who coordinates the tripod. The term "pod" is short for tripod and the terms are interchangeable. Everyone in the "pod" should have an opportunity to act as a tripod head. This makes it more difficult for the group to be compromised or sabotaged from the outside. It also gives everyone in the tripod an opportunity to really know what the "head" does, which should make it easier to help the "tripod head" help the group. Additionally, if a member of the pod is missing, the tripod can be quickly reconfigured to accomplish the mission.

Tripods should specialize in a particular pod activity. For example, there should be medical pods, communication pods, resource pods, art pods, data pods, helping pods, church pods, political pods, disruptor pods, etc. These are just examples. There are many ways to help people stay safe and sane while disrupting and neutralizing the machine so it can be repurposed for helping people instead of serving the sociopaths.

That said, just because one specializes in one thing does not mean the pod or its members are limited to one activity. Discovering, studying and practicing other pod tactics will enhance all pod tactics. Indeed, because many of the pod activities can and should become lifestyles and can be carried out independently, Asymmetrical Resistance Members can act as an independent pod. This kind of cross-fertilization of ideas and tactics adds to the randomness and asymmetry of the method, making it more effective.

Machines Versus People

Machines have advantages

Machines move slowly and deliberately. They have the advantage of mass and efficient coordination. They know more about us than we usually know about them. They can use this knowledge to make people operate against themselves. They can be more focused since they have fewer people to satisfy. Their need to subjugate us for their collective use is settled between their members and focused. They can, and do, discuss strategies to fill this need in small secret meetings and conferences. With little opposition, theycontrol most of the world's resources, including the most valuable of resources, its people.

They have something of a religious belief that "god" has given them dominion over the rest of us and that we need them and their descendants to control everyone and all of the resources. They often belong to religions that reinforce these bizarre hallucinations. This focus of purpose, wealth of resources and the ability to predict and control our actions to their advantage make opposition difficult, but not impossible.

Machines also have disadvantages

The sheer size of their operation makes The Machine unwieldy. It seems efficient because it has not met asymmetrical conditions. "The boulder seems balanced until the pebble that maintains the balance is removed".

Machines have a lot of considerations to make before changes can be made. Any neglected consideration creates an opportunity for malfunction or destruction. A complex system depends on many intricate operations that have limited tolerance for slack. The lack of slack is an inherent vulnerability. Read "Slack: Getting Past Burnout, Busywork, and the Myth of Total Efficiency" by Tom DeMarco to understand this.

The sufficiency of slack creates opportunities for the introduction of artifact. Being able to recognize and exploit these opportunities is key to the Asymmetrical Resistance Method.

For example, if the system depends on fear, hatred and competition to function, the degree to which these can be reduced or eliminated is the degree to which the machine will find it difficult to operate.

The larger the mass, the more difficult it is for machines to maneuver. With some notable exceptions they can be slow to respond to change or even be aware of change. Compare a motorcycle to a semi-truck or a jet ski to a battleship. Large machines depend on large numbers of people to feed and maintain them. Machines need people. People can benefit from machines but can also do quite well without them.

Machines depend on stable, relatively consistent environments. They have a difficult time adjusting to change. Small focused, asymmetrical changes, plus time, can immobilize machines or even make large machines self-destruct. These small changes can be made to machines or the environment in which they operate.

People have advantages

People create machines. People feed and maintain the machines so they actually control the machines. Individuals, with training, can move more quickly and adjust to changes more rapidly than machines. They can maneuver faster. They can act unpredictably, irrationally and asymmetrically, — that is to say they are more flexible. There are more people than there are large machines.

With training, people can operate independently of machines. People can self-adapt, without the assistance of machines.

A single, trained, disciplined individual can wreak havoc on a machine. Small teams can exponentially multiply the effectiveness with coordinated attacks.

One can blend in with the many, becoming essentially invisible. This opens an encyclopedia of actions while greatly reducing exposure to retaliation.

People also have disadvantages

Coordination can be a challenge for people. Understanding what other people are feeling or thinking is critical to coordination. People have a hard time figuring out what others are feeling or thinking. Worse, they often think they know what others are feeling or thinking.

People with little or no knowledge or concern for doing the most good, for the most people, most often can act in ways that destroy or disrupt life for everyone. The activities of these lone actors can become as great a problem as "The Machine". Lack of consensus as to what constitutes doing the most good, for the most people, most often inhibits coordination and cooperation. Arguments about this can feed The Machine and harm people.

People like patterns, and this makes it easy to anticipate and manipulate them. To make this method work we need to break our patterns on a more regular basis. Relook at everything, everyday. Do lots of thought experiments. Take another route home. Talk to total strangers. Listen to opposing views. Ask new questions. Travel to somewhere new. Take calculated risks with full consideration of the risk/reward ratio. Go to a different church. Call politicians. Volunteer with an organization you have never heard of or investigated. Say something nice to people whom you think/know hate you. Take a new class. Shop at a different store. In short, shake it up. Don't be predictable.

Many people have come to depend on the machine. They depend on it for critical resources, like food and water. They depend on the machine to tell them what to think and do. They depend on the machine for happiness. They are addicted to the machine. Fortunately this dependency is an illusion. The reality is that the machine depends on the people. People existed before the machine. People can exist if the machine is destroyed. People can thrive if they co-opt and repurpose The Machine to benefit the many, instead of a relatively few sociopaths.

The goal of this manual is to disrupt the machine in such a way as to make it subservient to the people that created and maintain it. Exploration on how this can be done is the subject of this Asymmetrical Resistance Manual, ARM.

Money Should Not Be Our Master

One reason for the unequal distribution of resources is the worshiping of wealth. Not only those with money who worship money, those who are victimized by the insatiable appetites of sociopaths for money also worship money.

We have a tendency to judge others according to what they have rather than what they attempt to contribute to the common good. When we judge people more on what they have than what kind of person they are or try to be, we allow money to be our master. When money is our master, those with the money become our masters. We become subject to the new "golden rule"; those with the gold, rule.

Money is just paper. In some cases it is merely digits on a hard disk somewhere. After obtaining a certain amount of money people don't become more happy if they get more money.

On the contrary, our new wealth level becomes our "new poverty level" and we feel the need to acquire more. We become more fearful of losing our new-found wealth. We often discover we have to find "new friends", leaving behind those who helped us succeed and whom we could trust in order to climb our new "social ladder". These "new friends" don't really want us in their club and will be looking for ways to make us fail and send us back down that social ladder. The cost for staying in our position will be to participate in the oppression of others. Do that well and you will be found useful enough to keep around. But you will be accepted only as a lap dog or guard dog. You will never be as much a part of their family as their actual dogs.

You can only live in so many houses, eat so much food, buy so much sex, spend so much money. So why do people want more, besides being chronically insecure and trying to escape reminders of their mortality?

Many people seek great wealth in order to feel they are superior to those with less, in other words very people that enable them to have the wealth.

Removing the motivation to make more money is an oil leak in the machine.

Some people want more money because they want people to be wowed and grovel at their feet. They want to feel others envy them. They want others to want to be them. They want to be worshipped. This can help support their illusion that they have greater value than others and are closer to "god" or worse, they feel closer to immortality.

They have attached their value to how much money they have or how many resources they control relative to others. It is not just how much they have that counts, it is how little others have relative to them. It is not so much that they should succeed, but that others should fail. Yes, these people are sick.

These mental and emotional illnesses form the basis for so much of the suffering people experience. One tactic to destabilize the machine is to reduce the power of money in our lives. We can refuse to let money be our master.

Starving this cancer is an important and somewhat easy first step in the Asymmetrical Resistance Method. It does not require anyone's permission or even agreement. It does not require dispossessing others of their money. It only requires that we simply stop showing deference to people based on how much money or which resources they possess. It requires that we ask how this person is doing the most good, for the most people, most often, rather than how much money do they have or what do they "own".

We can show social deference to those who make the effort to do the most good, for the most people, most often. We can give them strong, positive eye contact. We can give them smiles and warmth. We can watch their backs. We can give them the best table in a restaurant. We can reward them with invitations to special events. We can reward them with invitations into special social circles where special love is shown. We can vote for them. We can support their businesses or personal efforts. We can introduce them to special people. We show people special love who show others special love.

We must find ways to do things with as little money as possible. We must go beyond even bartering. We need to find ways to deliver goods and services with a minimum of money. We must find ways to elect officials with the least money possible. We must find ways to do projects with the least money possible.

One simple way to move in this direction is by giving away what we don't need or are not using. This involves creating a network that allows us to introduce everything we are not using into the emerging "free economy". Sites like https://www.freecycle.org/ provide examples of how to get what we are not using into the hands of those who could use it.

The sharing economy is another way to minimize the importance of money in our lives. https://en.wikipedia.org/wiki/Sharing_economy.

Donating to thrift stores that are trying to do the most good, for the most people, most often is also a good way to minimize the power of money. Hold or donate to garage or yard sales with proceeds going towards people or projects that seek to do the most good, for the most people, most often can also help.

Diminishing the meaning of money can mean doing favors for people while minimizing or eliminating the role of money in the transaction. The payment is akin to the feeling you get when you help your mother across the street. If you can't see why you wouldn't want to charge her for that, then this idea might not make much sense to you. If you can see that, then try to slowly expand the people and causes you would help without the expectation of compensation.

The more we can do things like this, the less money and people with it have power over us and the less we are slaves to money and those with it.

We can let kindness be our new currency.

We can do this by not groveling, ooing and awing about expensive things. We can cease to give people who are big tippers special treatment. We can refuse to treat people differently based on their wealth. We can judge people by how much good they do, for how many people and how often they do it. We can respect how well a person treats theirfamily, community and strangers rather than what kind of car they drive, house they live in or clothes they wear. We can practice not noticing or regarding with indifference extravagance or displays of wealth. We can lean toward making people more ashamed of their wealth than proud of it.

We can detach our own sense of self worth from the things we possess, or better put that possess us, or how much money we have.

The more we give deference to people based on their reputation for kindness and caring, the more we minimize the power of money. If more money can have less meaning, we can devalue money to the point where it can no longer be our master. When the money ceases to be our master, those with the money will cease to be our master.

Resource Pods (covered more thoroughly later) are a way to specialize in minimizing the power of money and those who have lots of it in our lives.

Removing the motivation to make more money is sand in "The Machine".

The Evolution Of Workers

Let's not serve those who seek to subjugate us.

We need to rethink our relationship with our employers. Too many of us undervalue our contribution to the individuals and enterprises we work for, not only in monetary terms but also in terms of the products or services they provide. We don't think we have anything to say about the policies they pursue or the politics they support.

We neglect the fact that many of these people and enterprises hold us in deep contempt. They make enough to share the profits with the workers who make their profits possible with little if any change in their opulent lifestyles. But they derive more satisfaction in how much misery they can inflict than in increased profits. They not only under pay workers, they create and/or maintain conditions they know are injuring or killing them. When workers complain they are fired. They break up unions that try to improve conditions. These people will spend more money to line the pockets of crooked politicians than it would take to improve workers lives. Sociopaths are just like that.

If you are being paid, it is quite likely because you add value in some way to the enterprise. Even though people speak in terms of giving people jobs, that is a mind trick. A job is not a gift. It is payment for services. If you are getting paid, money is being made from the contribution you make towards that company's success. If not, that company is likely looking for a way to get rid of you.

Workers deserve a share of that profit commensurate to the value they add to the enterprise.

If you make a contribution to a company and they take the profits and support people and causes that make your life or the lives of others miserable, then you are contributing to your problems and the problems of others.

It can no longer be just about how much money people are paid. We must consider our contributions to individuals and enterprises that make people miserable. We have to ask if and how our work contributes to doing the most good, for the most people most often. Is our work part of the solution or part of the problem?

We need to rethink how our actions help sociopaths succeed. All of the personal services like gardening, house cleaning, infant care, car washing, secretarial services, etc. free up time for sociopaths to think up new ways to make our lives miserable. When poor people service country clubs where no one who looks like them or comes from their neighborhoods can be a member, they are contributing to their own oppression. When, as part of their job, workers are expected to absorb insults large and small from sociopaths who think they are on a first name basis with god, that is a job that makes sure workers and their descendants will be subjugated to the role of "rented slave". These jobs, whatever they pay, are contributing to worker oppression.

Imagine if these sociopaths had to figure out and manage all of the things taken care of by the armies of people who they hold in contempt. Imagine if all the golf courses and country clubs and other "exclusive" places could no longer find people willing to work for any less than the attorneys and accountants and only on condition that all of the people they serve must serve others by doing the MOST good, for the MOST people, MOST often. If nothing else, these people would have less time to plot how to make the lives of others miserable.

Think of how the world would change if the thinking people of this world refused to help sociopaths succeed. Few individuals "create" wealth without a team of people. These teams of people usually contribute more ideas and energy than those who benefit.

Some company "owners" have a few good ideas, but they make more money from other people's ideas than they do from any ideas they alone dreamed up. And they can't realize these ideas without the contributions of others.

Sometimes owners or managers will encourage ideas from workers on the line with bonuses. Those small bonuses are a little pat on the head in exchange for an idea that the company will claim as its own, patent and make millions. If it is a labor-saving idea, someone, maybe even the person who came up with the idea, will lose their job.

Researchers spend hours positioning themselves to make new discoveries, taking most of the risk with experiments that are usually dead ends but point the way to success later. Success is built on failures. The researchers typically receive no compensation relative to the benefit the company derives from their discoveries.

When they discover something, people who have not taken any of the risk will often swoop in and take the credit and benefit. These "owners" then have the audacity to claim ownership of the ideas and the profits from the ideas. If researchers started to work collaboratively and hired sales, legal and marketing people rather than having sales, legal and marketing people hire them, they might get more benefit and respect.

It might be time for workers to rethink their value to companies. It is time for unions to get more creative. They need to take some of the union dues and purchase stock in the companies where they work. They can purchase a seat at the table where the decisions are really made cheaper than the cost of a strike. Over time and with strategic planning workrs could come to own the publicly traded companies where they work. Workers can better position themselves to rid themselves of greedy CEO's and help the other stockholders in the process. They could benefit from being on the same side of the negotiating table as stockholders and management. They would be better positioned to protect themselves from the sociopaths in these traditionally opposing groups.

Workers can share information about which companies and managers are good to work with and which ones are not. Workers can work hard to help companies that treat workers well succeed in the market place. Conversely they can do all kinds of legal things to make things difficult for companies that don't treat workers well.

Workers need to stop helping companies eliminate their jobs. It is often workers who transport, set up and train workers in low wage polluting countries. It is workers who buy the products that are made by companies that eliminated their jobs.

Workers have the power to make or break companies. They need to start using that power to clean up the labor marketplace.

Co-Opt the Cops

"Co-opt the Cops" is the part of the Asymmetrical Resistance Method that seeks to reduce the "fire power" of the machine by repurposing law enforcement and military to serve the people instead of "The Machine".

In too many cases the police and military have been co-opted by The Machine. Law enforcement should exist to serve ALL of the people. They should not be the enemy of the people. Underneath the uniforms are living breathing people. To be sure, such a profession can attract sociopaths looking for excitement. But that is a far cry from most cops being sociopaths.

That said, any cop can sometimes find himself or herself surrounded and manipulated by sociopaths. They can have a sociopathic superior or sociopathic partners. They can be subjected to people and frightening events that turn them bitter and hateful. But these police and military personnel are our brothers and sisters. We pay their salaries. We need them back, they are ours.   We need them on our side. They need us on their side. We need them doing the MOST good, for the MOST people, MOST often.

There are a number of ways to accomplish this. One is to show these people a little love. Hurt people, will hurt people. Cops are people. Even if some of them go out of their way to convince us they are not people, they are. Under those uniforms are living, breathing people with issues of their own. Even the corrupt, mentally sick, sadistic ones are still human.

The "Co-opt a Cop" strategy aims to reduce the tension between the people and law enforcement by getting to know cops on a personal level. Some ways to get this done:

Ask for their names instead of just their badge number. We can often get cops to act better by letting them know that we see them as people rather than a blood stained uniform or badge of dishonor.

Greet them warmly even when they are grumpy. Cops have bad days. They can often hide their humanity behind a scowl that covers their pain. Sometimes these grumpy faces hide the fact that they are in fear for their lives.   Making a safe space for them to take off their masks can have benefits for everyone.

Invite officers to community gatherings as people rather than police officers. If we want them to see us as human, we are going to have to put some effort into seeing police officers as human.

We all have flaws. We often have jobs and responsibilities that present situations and issues that go beyond our ability to cope. We can help police to help us by providing an environment that makes it easier to be a good cop than a bad one. That is co-opting the cops.

We can be especially cooperative with officers who show the community respect and act in a professional manner. Write letters of praise for an officer who acts professionally. Send them a copy. If you can find out their birthday, send or give them a birthday card from the community signed by as many people from the community as possible. Create a fund to present awards, plaques etc. that recognize the work and value of good police officers. Take out newspaper ads to praise exceptional or consistently good conduct by officers.

Watch the back of officers who earn the respect of the community. We especially need to protect those people. Their names should be known to the community. If they are transferred, complain loudly. Ask for them back. Little by little build a police force in your community that truly belongs to the community. Create an informal way for police officers to complain to the community when they feel disrespected as officers and create ways for those complaints to be addressed. Create a way for police to suggest ways they could better serve the community. In short, make a place in the community for police who want to be part of the community.

Write letters suggesting professional help for those who seem sociopathic and/or "off the chain". Establish community awards for outstanding service by a police officer. Report graft and corruption. When there is an officer who shows signs of mental illness, request a meeting with the head of the police department with a group of people (three-10) to suggest that the officer get treatment or be relieved of duty. Come to the meeting with specific complaints and evidence. Ask that the officer be transferred out of your community. If the head of the police department is uncooperative or shows signs of mental illness, request a meeting with the mayor or police commission to discuss the problem officer. It is best to have these conversations when tempers are not flaring. Keep notes of your effort in case legal or political action is required to get action.

When and if there is no improvement, then these issues and efforts should be brought up to elected officials. Groom and run candidates who have been groomed to replace unresponsive politicians.

Young people should be groomed to replace bad police officers. Sometimes these officers are tolerated because no one else wants the job and police departments need warm bodies. When those people are part of your community, they should truly be your police, rather than an occupying force serving the interests of sociopaths.

These are not the only tactics. They just form a template to get the discussion started on how to connect law enforcement with the communities they are sworn to serve rather than allow them to be an occupying force for sociopaths. We can't let the sociopaths win.

Clean Up the Economic System

Have you ever noticed that people have an allergy to any economic system that seeks to do the most good, for the most people, most often?

Many of these systems have been subverted and sabotaged from inside and out. But we should focus on the objectives and try to develop one that does the most good, for the most people, most often. The ones we have now fail at that. They usually see that as undesirable. Many people don't know if they are doing well without comparing their condition to what others have. Sociopaths need someone to suffer, otherwise they can't feel successful.

Exactly what that system is, is yet to be discovered or devised. But if we keep doing the most good, for the most people, most often, we can crowd-control its development and operation. In the mean time here are a few things we can do.

Move our money from banks to community credit unions.

Start community investment clubs that fund enterprise aimed at doing the most good, for the most people, most often. These clubs can be funded with the money people save by quitting bad habits such as gambling, smoking, drinking etc. They can be funded by activities like bake sales, car washes, garage/yard sales and other fundraisers. Many people don't have money to invest but, "extra" money can be pooled and used to fund local people who want to start businesses that aim to do the most good, for the most people, most often. This can take a bit of sophistication, but help is out here.

People can start buying clubs that can trade information on which products work and don't work. They can buy in bulk and wholesale. They can trade information about how to get the most use from products. They can form informal tool-lending groups so that everyone doesn't have to buy a tool, cooking device or book that they rarely use. They can car pool. They can watch for sales and let members know about them. They can keep notes on which companies do the most good, for the most people, most often and make an effort to buy from them.

The Tripods: Where The Rubber Meets The Road

The Helping Pod

Helping Pods can be thought of as the mortar that holds all of the other activities in the Asymmetrical Resistance Method together. They embody most directly what makes this approach feasible. The central idea behind their work is to be of help to others and make people feel good about themselves and others. When people feel good about themselves and others, they will be able to help one another and work together. When they work together and create something together, they will fear one another less. If they are less fearful, they will be much less vulnerable to those who would use their fear to destroy each other.

All pods should incorporate these basic principles into their work. It will help accomplish their missions. For example, if you listen intently to people who don't share your point of view, you will get more people to listen to you. If people who are not part of your pod feel a connection to you, they are more likely to cooperate with your mission. You will often need this cooperation.

If there is a kind of pod that might be considered the "most important", it would be The Helping Pod.

Rather than give a long complex explanation of what these pods do, here are some examples of the kinds of activities these pods could engage in. Because the whole point is to hide the needle in a stack of other needles, that is to say, to be anonymous and asymmetrical, this should be viewed as suggestions to get you started. You will need to improvise.

- Smile and be friendly to everyone
- Commit random acts of kindness
- Take food to those who are sick, shut in, or lacking food
- Give rides to people who lack transportation
- Help find solutions to people's problems
- Be there to listen to people who need a friendly ear
- Hold small parties in a fun atmosphere to get people together in a fun atmosphere who would not otherwise know one another
- Hold house parties to spread ideas that help people do the most good, for the most people, most often
- Cheer people up (spread joy)

- Give refuge to those who are in danger
- Seek out and interview people with opposing views. Record them when possible to bring up their points of view in discussion groups. These are useful to refine your own views as well as to shape your message to people when sharing opposing views. You have to listen if you want to be heard.
- Send greeting cards to those who are sick, have birthdays or might otherwise feel left out and lonely
- Make introductions
- Help people find friends
- Volunteer when there is a disaster
- Learn and be ready to use First Aid or other emergency care
- Provided 24/7 bailout phone number for people to call in case of an emergency.
- Develop and keep updated a resource directory for all kinds of emergencies
- Crowdsource solutions
- Network with others
- Help others start Helping Pods
- If you are religious, start prayer circles
- Create a petty cash fund to handle small emergencies

In short, Helping Pods find needs and fill them.

For insight on how to develop these skills I recommend "How to Win Friends and Influence People" by Dale Carnegie.

Art Pods

Art pods have great value to the Asymmetrical Resistance Method. They can help communicate complex ideas and feelings with art. They can provide activities that people who don't know one another can do together to create bonding opportunities. And the art they produce can be therapeutic to a whole community.

Art Tripods should not be limited to "professionals". Everyone who wants to do art can create or work with an Art Tripod.

Artists Tripods can:

- Create art that teaches love and kindness
- Create bright pictures and colors to uplift a community
- Create art with visions of people working together
- Put on performances like plays, skits and poetry that encourage people to work together for a better world
- Write and perform songs that encourage people to work together for a better world
- Write narratives, books, short stories, and poetry that illustrate how people can work together for a better world
- Create murals that tell stories or make statements that encourage people to work together for a better world
- Make banners and signs for protests
- Make T-shirts, car magnets, buttons, post cards and greeting cards with messages that get people focused
- Create art that encourages people to keep up the struggle
- Teach art to others so that their efforts can be multiplied.

In short, Art Tripods can make art with a mission and a message. The ways art can be used in the Asymmetrical Resistance Method are limited only by the imagination. Artists should have plenty of that.

Data Pods

The Data Pod is a kind of nerve center of the Asymmetrical Resistance Method. It specializes in gathering, vetting and storing information. It seeks to sort facts from "alternative facts", otherwise know as bald-faced lies. To that end it engages in these kinds of activities.

- Collect and share stories of people's lives
- Control rumors
- Fact check
- Gather and store images that tell stories
- Identify and maintain databases from various sources
- Make hard copies of critical data
- Share stories with art and communication pods
- Support the communication pods
- Put selected files on CDs, DVDs and Flash/Thumb drives to allow for distribution.

- Put larger files on CD's, DVDs and Flash/Thumb drives. These devices make it easier to backup, store and distribute data.
- Make hard copies of critical information. These can be used to compare electronic versions to see if alterations have been made. It also makes data retrieval possible when power is interrupted. If you have the capability, consider using laser etching to make hard copies of critical info.

Expect that your system will eventually be compromised despite your best efforts. You might consider a computer that cannot be connected to the Internet and limit access to any but those with access keys/passwords. Cloning your data system will allow you to get back up quickly.

Communication Pod

The Communication Pod takes information gathered by a Data Pod and finds ways to disseminate it. It can be thought of as a public relations or marketing unit. Members need not have experience in sales, marketing and public relations but the pod could benefit from people who are experienced in those businesses. A pod of people who are all highly experienced and creative can be especially effective. These pods can benefit from having graphic artists, web/computer techies, social media savvy techies etc. in the group. Having a good connection to an Art Pod could also be beneficial.

Here are a few examples of activities a Communication Pod [Com-Pod] can engage in.

- Develop communication phone-tree to send out important messages and call people into action
  - The phone tree is set up in multiples of 10.   [That is to say each person calls 10 people and each one of those people calls another 10 people into infinity. Make sure that two or more of the calls go to numbers external to the starting country.]
  - Each person should know the 10 people on their list.
  - They should remind each person to call their list soon.
  - Add redundancy into each branch of the tree of two to three people, i.e., there should be some over lapping.
  - Add artifact into your list (put in extra people on the list who are not actually called by list owners. An artifact number might be called by someone who doesn't know the list. This call will serve as a signal that your list has been compromised)

- Assume your list is compromised
- Meet regularly with your tripod members
- Vet information before putting it into your communication tree
- Document any information before putting it into your phone tree
- Test the list quarterly
- The tree can be duplicated with an email list, but the email list is easier to hack or shut down. Use the phone, preferably land lines.
- Create grapevines to spread general information virally
    - Talk to strangers. More importantly, ask them leading questions
    - Drop comments, one liners
    - Send postcards with hand-written messages fewer than 140 chracters
    - Send greeting cards with slogans fewer than 140 chracters
    - Print short runs of business cards with messages or slogans or other information with fewer than 140 characters
- Find multiple channels to pass information and fill the channels with information. Here are some suggested channels.
    - Email
    - Postal Service
    - Podcasts
    - Books
    - Pamphlets
    - Messages on business cards
    - YouTube
    - Movies made on iPhones
    - Photos
    - All parties with movies and discussions
    - Discussion groups
    - Concerts and performances

When using these channels and any others you may think of, make sure you try to spread the messages to other countries. This will make it harder for Machines to filter, edit or shut down messages. Make translations when possible.

At lot of people in media are facing hard times. There could come a time in the near future when they will begin to be prosecuted, persecuted or assassinated in the United States as they are in other countries. There needs to be a place for these journalists to publish articles that are thoroughly vetted but are "too hot" for traditional media. Journalists should be known to the pod. Perhaps pseudonyms could be used to shield the reporter.

The credibility of the pod is critical. Every effort should be made to maintain that credibility; however, there will be stories that turn out to be less than accurate. When that happens, issue quick corrections or retractions in plain view, with an apology. If a reporter develops a pattern of getting things wrong, let them go. Credibility is hard to gain and easy to lose.

Put larger files on CD's, DVDs and flash/thumb drives.

Make hard copies of critical information. These can be used to compare electronic versions to see if alterations have been made. If you have the capability, consider using laser etching to print critical information.

Create talking points. Many people want to help you spread the word but lack the ability to communicate effectively. You can help them by giving them talking points.

Provide public speaking coaching. Many people are terrified of speaking in public. With a little practice many people can greatly improve their public speaking ability. Some of them might even get comfortable enough to run for public office. Groom those people.

Religious Pods

People who want to do the most good, for the most people, most often have allowed sociopaths who are "pimping" their religion to define what their religion is about. Religions that want to do the most good, for the most people, most often can push their way back to the center of the social and political stage by boldly taking their messages of love and compassion to that stage. They can no longer afford to be silent and let their religion be defined by the more vocal sociopaths.

The religious pods can be quite effective, especially for people who work better when working with their God. Each faith has a different approach so they will need to find a style that works best for them. Some suggested approaches would be:

- Organize prayer vigils. Most faiths hold that prayer is central to the practice of their faith.
- Quietly standing still in large groups can be quite effective.

- Long silent single file candle light marches with religious symbols can demonstrate interest in a cause. They can also draw new people to a cause. This kind of march can be defined by its length of distance and/or time.
- Use the status of your faith to help people work together to serve the common good.
- Teach the good things your faith teaches that help people find and maintain their humanity.
- Connect and create fellowship with those of other faiths seeking to do the MOST good, for the MOST people, MOST often.
- Organized interfaith activities
- Organize peace making activities
- Create conflict resolution teams
- Write faith-based letters to politicians, news media, business owners etc.

These are just a few suggestions to get you started. Religious pods might find value in creating a "faith-based" pod that performs the actions of some of the other pods. There is lots of room for innovation.

Political Pod

The Political Pod is concerned with analyzing politicians and political policies for how they provide the MOST good, for the MOST people, MOST often [3Ms]. To that end they do things like:

- Recruit, cultivate and groom people for political office
- Keep files on politicians, political groups and legislation
- Analyze the impact of political actions on people
- Organize political action around the 3Ms
- Provide political support for 3M candidates
- Rate 3M candidates:
    - 0   =   never helps people
    - M   =   rarely helps people
    - MM   =   Sometimes helps people
    - MMM   =   Always helps people
- Maintain list of phone numbers of political operatives
- Suggest political actions
- Register voters
- Collect signatures for ballot issues and candidates

- Ferret out political lies and distortions in interviews and public statement and publicize them. Bring these up when politicians come to talk to their constituents.
- Analyze the words and actions of politicians. Write papers, create YouTube videos and podcasts and publicize these on public media.
- Publically hold politicians accountable. E.g., in public meetings, coordinate to re-ask questions that politicians dodge or ask follow-up questions to the same questions.

Resource Pod

Even in poor places there are wasted resources. These resources can be material. They can be human. They can be intellectual. They can be spiritual. Resources come in many forms.

The purpose of a Resource Pod is to locate, repurpose and redistribute resources.

To this end Resource Pods:

- Identify and classify resources
- Set up a Freecycle service https://www.freecycle.org/
- Classify resources from critical to frivolous so that they can be located and redistributed
- Identify surplus and deficits of resources
- Find ways to move resources without money
- Create crowd-sourced investment pools to fund projects that help the most people most often
- Create list of Employee Friendly Businesses (EFB) and publicize the list. Urge people to support these businesses by working for them and buying their goods and services.
- Create a list of businesses with good customer service and good products and services. Publicize the list. Urge people to support these businesses by working for them and buying their goods and services.
- Support economic unity in the world community
- Create list of businesses that have a positive impact on the natural environment. Publicize the list. Urge people to support these businesses by working for them and buying their goods and services.

- Crowd source money to fund investor groups that invest in ideas that help people and make profits. Reinvest profits to expand clout. Each investor gets one vote. These groups can also fund local small businesses.
- Crowd source money to fund investor groups that invest in publicly traded companies in order to influence their policies. Stock ownership also creates access to inside information. In many cases objections to policies can be raised at stockholder meetings.
- Crowd source money to save people from foreclosure or repossession.
- Help people with bankruptcy and other economic problems.

In short, the Resource Pod knows where to get stuff, who needs stuff and how to get stuff where it is most needed for the best price. It knows how to minimize the need for money and put this knowledge to work to do the most good, for the most people, most often.

It will be useful to the Resource Pod to familiarize itself with the concepts of the "shared economy".

https://en.wikipedia.org/wiki/Sharing_economy

The Sharing Economy: The End of Employment and the Rise of Crowd-Based Capitalism by Arun Sundararajan

Using this concept, it is possible to explore methods to minimize waste and the need for money while maximizing sharing and use of natural resources.

Disruptor Pods

The Disruptor Pods are the Asymmetrical Resistance Method's alternative to public demonstrations. They operate mostly hidden in plain view. Their purpose is to cause disruptions to doing "business as usual" while minimizing damage to people, property and People Friendly Businesses (PFB) in order to immobilize and/or repurpose The Machine.

The disruptor pod is used to disrupt, but never to destroy. It can do so by temporarily but asymmetrically disrupting traffic. It can compound the disruption by attacking multiple sites in an asymmetrical pattern of time, place and tactics. The disruptor pods should be used for focused demonstrations with minimal exposure to more vulnerable people.

Done correctly, these tactics could bring cities and government to a grinding halt. This is not usually desirable. But in the case of extreme regimes, these activities could be critical to neutralizing the power of sociopaths.

Impede The Machine

If people jump out in front of the machine, they will usually just get crushed. It is better to introduce a bit of sand into the gears and allow time to do the damage. It is better to loosen or remove a small screw that is likely to be overlooked and let the subsequent vibration shake The Machine apart over time. It is better to change the terrain in such a way that it damages The Machine, preferably in a way that is imperceptible to The Machine.

Attack the articulations and weak points rather than expending a lot of emotional energy entertaining sociopaths who are looking for a chance to bash your brains out.

Examples

These examples are only meant to be examples and templates. They have been culled from many tactics, some of which are thought to be too "effective" for the "uninitiated." Crowd and pod sourcing, personal and crowd-sourced experience, brainstorming and your imagination will be the well from which the best ideas will be drawn.

Recall that The Machine depends on us fearing it and mistrusting one another. Every attempt to reduce fear and mistrust between people is sand in the gears of the machine. Every degree to which we can replace the motivation for people to commit random acts of violence with the will to commit random acts of kindness adds metal chips to the transmission of the machine. Every ounce of the blood and bones of our mothers, brothers, fathers and sisters we refuse to surrender to the jaws of The Machine, will be starving The Machine of its sociopathic fuel.

To that end, asymmetric resistance minimizes the value of mass demonstrations in favor of asymmetrical targeted attacks aimed at maximum disruption of the machine with minimum destruction to people and property.

The machine needs efficiency. It needs the people it is chewing up in order to keep running. When supplies are late, information is slow and unreliable, and/or people arrive stressed and unhappy, it is impeded. Its ability to function is diminished. When these things happen randomly but often, The Machine can find it nearly impossible to adjust to such unpredictability.

Large ships move and turn slowly. They depend on rapidly and smoothly spinning gears to keep moving. Disrupting the gears, even a little, can have great benefit when done randomly but persistently. This can be done by "introducing artifact into the algorithm". Basically this means introducing small and if possible imperceptible, disruptions into the system.

The fact that they are small and random, makes them difficult to detect and/or analyze. They can easily be written off as "artifact" or "anomalies". Solutions to what seem to be "one time" events are maddening to system analysts. The importance of not creating a pattern can't be over stressed.

Instead of hundreds or thousands of people marching on freeways, stage automobile breakdowns at strategic locations. Maximize the effectiveness of this disruption with multiple breakdowns that could be staged for about the same time in far-flung areas of a city. The calculation should take into account how many tow trucks are available. It should be planned to take advantage of already recurring traffic problems.

Make a little problem big. Make a big problem bigger. Hide the needle in a stack of other needles.

Points to keep in mind

- Use different cars with different problems so as to mask the attack.
- Use different people.
- Inclement weather in poor visibility at times of dense traffic can amplify the effect.
- Pulling off the side of the road can cause rubbernecking. This can be nearly as effective as a traffic stall. "Naturally occurring" smoke can increase the effectiveness of this tactic. But the use of things like smoke bombs to make the smoke makes you suspect. You want to hide in plain view.

In addition to a Boycott

- Take more time to do everything
- Be clumsy and waste time at the checkout lines
- Make mistakes
- Have large numbers of people go into a store dressed so they can be confused as employees

- Have large numbers of people "shop" at the same time. Don't all shop at the same time. Don't act in unison in any way. Use up all the carts. Take hours to "shop" at the busiest shopping time. Abandon the carts.
- Slowly fumble to make payments
- Decide you don't want things just after they have been scanned
- If you must bag your items yourself do it slowly. Put things in your bag, then take them out and rearrange them. The store will need to have people come and help you or just wait or have people go around you.
- The objective is to create long lines and cause people to give up and drop their purchases.
- Hide in plain view. Make it random. Make it difficult for the store or government to retaliate without retaliating against other "real" customers. This is a denial of service attack.

Communication System Disruption

Communication is the nervous system of The Machine. Call flooding can be a tactic. Pick a time and target and have people call at the same time. Have calls come from various places since calls from one location, even with cell phones, can be located and potentially blocked or stopped.

Keeping in mind that asymmetry is key: Randomize the attack. For example make the call attack for 34 minutes, stop it for 15, attack for 17 minutes, stop 45, attack for 60, stop for 10, attack for 13 etc. This can be done for a day or a week, a year or forever. Just keep it random. Different phone numbers. Different people. Different companies.

This can be used effectively on companies or politicians that rely on telephone communications.

Flash Mobbing

Large crowds can make a statement about the popularity of a movement. It is hard to say that people don't care about something when people are protesting in the street. It is also a place where like-minded people can meet. Large groups are also vulnerable to crazies who provoke/spark violence and police retaliation. They present an opportunity to send in provocateurs to cause trouble and justify police action. For that reason large groups are better suited for things like prayer and candle light vigils and silent marches.

That said, there are other effective ways to protest.

Instead of large groups in one location, the asymmetrical approach takes advantage of the relative difficulty of moving in police or military units to break up protests. Groups should be broken into smaller groups whose numbers fall below the threshold that require a permit. The lack of a permitting requirement allows for the rapid deployment of small groups that can disrupt activities and make continuing doing business as usual difficult.

The activities should use "disrupt and disappear" tactics. That is to say, carry out disruptive activities below the level of "criminal activity" and then dissolve or disappear at the appearance or request of the police. Then go to another place and repeat the same activity. Create these disruptions in key places that create mobilization problems for The Machine. You should not create the mobilization problems. They should just exist and you take advantage of them.

Think through your action plan. Eliminate anything that could be the direct cause of bodily injury or property damage. Have a bail-out plan and attorneys identified and available in case of legal challenges. Take pictures and videos, not for publication, but for legal protection. If your picture is all over YouTube, you can't very well be a needle hiding in a stack of other needles.

Eventually the police will know who you are. They have cameras as well. This is why you need to operate within the letter of the law. If you are arrested, it should be easy to get your charges dismissed.

DO NOT resist police. Disperse before they even ask you. And don't run. As long as you are "un-arrested", you are available to "pop up" somewhere else. Do so. Stay random. If they say "Don't do that thing again"…don't for now. Do another thing that disrupts instead.

Flash Mobs of Disruptor Pods of 10 people can make spontaneous appearances in places with T-shirts and placards. They can walk around at major intersections, disrupting but not permanently blocking traffic. At the slightest hint that law-enforcement is showing up they should calmly disband, but reassemble at some other predetermined location to repeat the same action. Never run away from police. Act friendly with them and treat them with respect. Try to get them on your side. Refer to them as brother/sister or officer (refer back to Co-opt a Cop).

These tactics can be augmented by people dancing or wrestling in Gorilla suits or staging bikini pageants. You could also have a Pod wear Halloween costumes when it is not Halloween. The freakier the better. Just walking along the street or dancing with placards in an unorganized fashion works well. Try holding a disco with no music. The objective is to cause distractions to slow things down while drawing attention to a cause without actually staging a "protest". Try to give the people a good feeling with these tactics. Brighten their day while educating them.

Every attempt should be made to avoid adversarial contact with law enforcement. The goal is to slow down traffic, not stop it. This action carried on at multiple sites throughout the city should have a larger impact than one large demonstration in one place in the city only seen on the nightly news. It is also important to try and call attention to an issue without getting people enraged. You want people to view your cause favorably.

Slowing down things for seconds turns into minutes that turn into chaos. This often happens "naturally". You want to go with this flow. Hide the needle in a stack of other needles. Act randomly. Make a big problem bigger. Disrupt and disappear.

In the big picture you make it difficult for the system to work.

Flash mobs come in many flavors. They can come with placards. They can come with songs. They can come with dancing. They can come beating on pots and pans in and rhythms and chanting. They can be eerily silent standing still with vacant stares. They can stage skits and plays in public places. They can hold spontaneous prayer vigils. The number of activities the flash mobs can engage in is limited only by the imagination.

The Machine depends on people being uncoordinated. To that end it needs people to be suspicious of one another. It needs people to be competitive with one another. It needs people to view the world through a zero sum lens. It takes advantage of the neurological limits of the number of relationships each person can maintain to limit people's ability to bond and realize their common interests.

This strategy depends on the people neutralizing this power. To coordinate an asymmetric attack on The Machine, the people must find a way to connect to their common humanity. People must trade in their limited tribal identities to the greater identity of the greater human family.

The degree to which people are able to do this is the degree to which they can't be manipulated by The Machine to destroy one another.

The strategy to do this starts with a simple concept: "refuse to be enemies". While fundamentally simple, most people have been reprogrammed to fear one another. This barrier must be overcome if asymmetrical resistance is to be successful because asymmetric resistance requires a lot of "wink and nod", intuitive human communication that machines find hard to decipher.

Imagine a dance hall where the song changes but the dancers are able to improvise intuitively because they can "feel" the other dancers. While some will undoubtedly miss some beats, in a few beats the dancers will adjust because they want to dance and they are bonded by dance.

In order to bond in this way, humans need to dance with as many other humans as possible as often as possible. To dance means to do things together. To dance means to build and create things together. To dance means to freely give smiles or commit random acts of kindness to any other human as often as possible. To dance means to make great effort to leave no one behind. To dance means to commit to a mutual protection pact with all of humanity. To dance means to add a non-compete clause to our contract with humanity. The dance means to realize, live and dance the mantra "we are all in this together."

Using these examples, you should be able to come up with your own tactics. Be creative. Just keep in mind it's about disruption, not destruction. Even sociopaths are our brothers and sisters. They are sick. They need love too. But we simply must impede their ability to make life miserable for others.

We can't let the sociopaths win.

Always look to do the MOST GOOD, for the MOST PEOPLE, Most OFTEN.

Glossary

ARM

- Asymmetrical Resistance Movement
- Asymmetrical Resistance Manual
- Asymmetrical Resistance MAP [Mutual Assistance People (Person)]
- Asymmetrical Resistance Method

Machine

Organizations, private or public, that act against the interest of humanity.

3M [MMM]

The gold standard of whether something is worthy of support by humans. A person, politician, policy, law, act, product that does the MOST good, for the MOST people, MOST often.

Tripod

The basic operational unit of asymmetrical resistance method. It consists of small groups of three that are are grouped into three pods plus one rotating head chosen by the group. Everyone should have an opportunity to act as a head. This makes it more difficult for the group to be compromised from the outside. It also gives everyone in the tripod an opportunity to know intimately what it means to be the "head", which should make it easier for everyone to help the group succeed in its missions.

Blow back = A term originating from within the (American) Intelligence community, denoting the unintended consequences, the unwanted (side-)effects or suffered repercussions of a covert operation that fall back on those responsible for the aforementioned operations. To the civilians suffering the blowback of covert operations, the effect typically manifests itself as "random" acts of political violence without a discernible, direct cause; because the public—in whose name the intelligence agency acted—are unaware of the effected secret attacks that provoked revenge (counter-attack) against them. From Wikipedia

More Information

https://en.wikipedia.org/wiki/Sharing_economy.

https://www.freecycle.org/

http://free.com/where-to-find-free-stuff-online

http://www.historyisaweapon.com/zinnapeopleshistory.html

https://zinnedproject.org/about/howard-zinn/

http://www.pbs.org/race/000_General/000_00-Home.htm

https://www.youtube.com/watch?v=B7_YHur3G9g

A People's History of the United States Reissue Edition by Howard Zinn

The Sociopath Next Door by Martha Stout

Slack: Getting Past Burnout, Busywork, and the Myth of Total Efficiency"
by Tom DeMarco

The Sharing Economy: The End of Employment and the Rise of Crowd-Based
Capitalism by Arun Sundararajan